The Successful Human's

Daily Planner and Note Taker

Activinotes

Activinotes

DAILY JOURNALS, PLANNERS, NOTEBOOKS AND OTHER BLANK BOOKS

Daily Planner and Note Taker

date
___

time	task	comments	status

to do list:

notes:

- ☐
- ☐
- ☐
- ☐
- ☐
- ☐
- ☐
- ☐
- ☐
- ☐
- ☐
- ☐
- ☐

Daily Planner and Note Taker

date
_____

time	task	comments	status

to do list:

notes:

- ☐
- ☐
- ☐
- ☐
- ☐
- ☐
- ☐
- ☐
- ☐
- ☐
- ☐
- ☐
- ☐

Daily Planner and Note Taker

date
_____

time	task	comments	status

to do list:

notes:

Daily Planner and Note Taker

date
___

time	task	comments	status

to do list:

notes:

□
□
□
□
□
□
□
□
□
□
□
□
□

Daily Planner and Note Taker

date
___

time	task	comments	status

to do list:

notes:

Daily Planner and Note Taker

date
___

time	task	comments	status

to do list:

notes:

- ☐
- ☐
- ☐
- ☐
- ☐
- ☐
- ☐
- ☐
- ☐
- ☐
- ☐
- ☐
- ☐

Daily Planner and Note Taker

date
___

time	task	comments	status

to do list:

notes:

- ☐
- ☐
- ☐
- ☐
- ☐
- ☐
- ☐
- ☐
- ☐
- ☐
- ☐
- ☐
- ☐
- ☐

Daily Planner and Note Taker

date
___

time	task	comments	status

to do list:

notes:

- ☐
- ☐
- ☐
- ☐
- ☐
- ☐
- ☐
- ☐
- ☐
- ☐
- ☐
- ☐
- ☐
- ☐

Daily Planner and Note Taker

date
___

time	task	comments	status

to do list:

notes:

☐
☐
☐
☐
☐
☐
☐
☐
☐
☐
☐
☐
☐
☐

Daily Planner and Note Taker

date ___

time	task	comments	status

to do list:

notes:

☐
☐
☐
☐
☐
☐
☐
☐
☐
☐
☐
☐

Daily Planner and Note Taker

date _____

time	task	comments	status

to do list:

notes:

Daily Planner and Note Taker

date
___

time	task	comments	status

to do list:

notes:

☐
☐
☐
☐
☐
☐
☐
☐
☐
☐
☐
☐
☐

Daily Planner and Note Taker

date
___

time	task	comments	status

to do list:

notes:

☐
☐
☐
☐
☐
☐
☐
☐
☐
☐
☐
☐
☐

Daily Planner and Note Taker

date
_____

time	task	comments	status

to do list:

notes:

- ☐
- ☐
- ☐
- ☐
- ☐
- ☐
- ☐
- ☐
- ☐
- ☐
- ☐
- ☐
- ☐
- ☐

Daily Planner and Note Taker

date
_____

time	task	comments	status

to do list:

notes:

- ☐
- ☐
- ☐
- ☐
- ☐
- ☐
- ☐
- ☐
- ☐
- ☐
- ☐
- ☐
- ☐

Daily Planner and Note Taker

date
_____

time	task	comments	status

to do list:

notes:

Daily Planner and Note Taker

date
___

time	task	comments	status

to do list:

notes:

- ☐
- ☐
- ☐
- ☐
- ☐
- ☐
- ☐
- ☐
- ☐
- ☐
- ☐
- ☐
- ☐

Daily Planner and Note Taker

date
_____

time	task	comments	status

to do list:

notes:

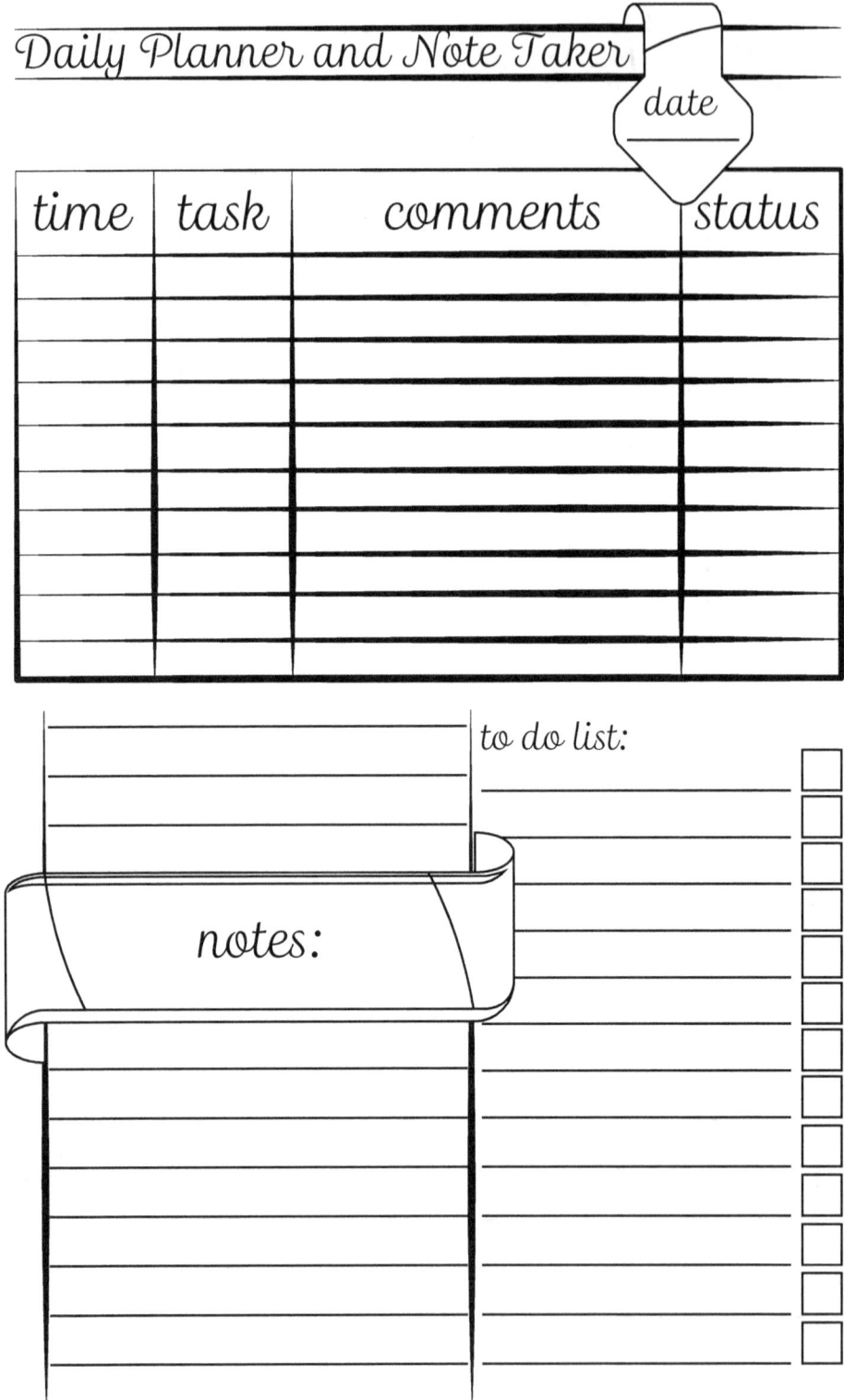

Daily Planner and Note Taker

date
___

time	task	comments	status

to do list:

notes:

Daily Planner and Note Taker

date
___

time	task	comments	status

to do list:

notes:

Daily Planner and Note Taker

date
___

time	task	comments	status

to do list:

notes:

- ☐
- ☐
- ☐
- ☐
- ☐
- ☐
- ☐
- ☐
- ☐
- ☐
- ☐
- ☐
- ☐

Daily Planner and Note Taker

date ____

time	task	comments	status

to do list:

notes:

- ☐
- ☐
- ☐
- ☐
- ☐
- ☐
- ☐
- ☐
- ☐
- ☐
- ☐
- ☐
- ☐

Daily Planner and Note Taker

date
_____

time	task	comments	status

to do list:

notes:

- ☐
- ☐
- ☐
- ☐
- ☐
- ☐
- ☐
- ☐
- ☐
- ☐
- ☐
- ☐
- ☐

Daily Planner and Note Taker

date _____

time	task	comments	status

to do list:

notes:

Daily Planner and Note Taker

date

time	task	comments	status

to do list:

notes:

Daily Planner and Note Taker

date
___

time	task	comments	status

to do list:

notes:

- ☐
- ☐
- ☐
- ☐
- ☐
- ☐
- ☐
- ☐
- ☐
- ☐
- ☐
- ☐
- ☐

Daily Planner and Note Taker

date
___

time	task	comments	status

to do list:

notes:

☐
☐
☐
☐
☐
☐
☐
☐
☐
☐
☐
☐
☐

Daily Planner and Note Taker

date ___

time	task	comments	status

to do list:

notes:

- ☐
- ☐
- ☐
- ☐
- ☐
- ☐
- ☐
- ☐
- ☐
- ☐
- ☐
- ☐
- ☐
- ☐

Daily Planner and Note Taker

date
___

time	task	comments	status

to do list:

notes:

Daily Planner and Note Taker

date
___

time	task	comments	status

to do list:

notes:

☐
☐
☐
☐
☐
☐
☐
☐
☐
☐
☐
☐
☐

Daily Planner and Note Taker

date
___

time	task	comments	status

to do list:

notes:

- ☐
- ☐
- ☐
- ☐
- ☐
- ☐
- ☐
- ☐
- ☐
- ☐
- ☐
- ☐
- ☐

Daily Planner and Note Taker

date
___

time	task	comments	status

to do list:

notes:

- ☐
- ☐
- ☐
- ☐
- ☐
- ☐
- ☐
- ☐
- ☐
- ☐
- ☐
- ☐
- ☐
- ☐

Daily Planner and Note Taker

date ___

time	task	comments	status

to do list:

- ☐
- ☐
- ☐
- ☐
- ☐
- ☐
- ☐
- ☐
- ☐
- ☐
- ☐
- ☐

notes:

Daily Planner and Note Taker

date
___

time	task	comments	status

to do list:

notes:

☐
☐
☐
☐
☐
☐
☐
☐
☐
☐
☐
☐
☐

Daily Planner and Note Taker

date ____

time	task	comments	status

to do list:

- ☐
- ☐
- ☐
- ☐
- ☐
- ☐
- ☐
- ☐
- ☐
- ☐
- ☐
- ☐
- ☐

notes:

Daily Planner and Note Taker

date
___

time	task	comments	status

to do list:

notes:

- ☐
- ☐
- ☐
- ☐
- ☐
- ☐
- ☐
- ☐
- ☐
- ☐
- ☐
- ☐
- ☐

Daily Planner and Note Taker

date
_____

time	task	comments	status

to do list:

notes:

- [ ]
- [ ]
- [ ]
- [ ]
- [ ]
- [ ]
- [ ]
- [ ]
- [ ]
- [ ]
- [ ]
- [ ]
- [ ]

Daily Planner and Note Taker

date _____

time	task	comments	status

to do list:

notes:

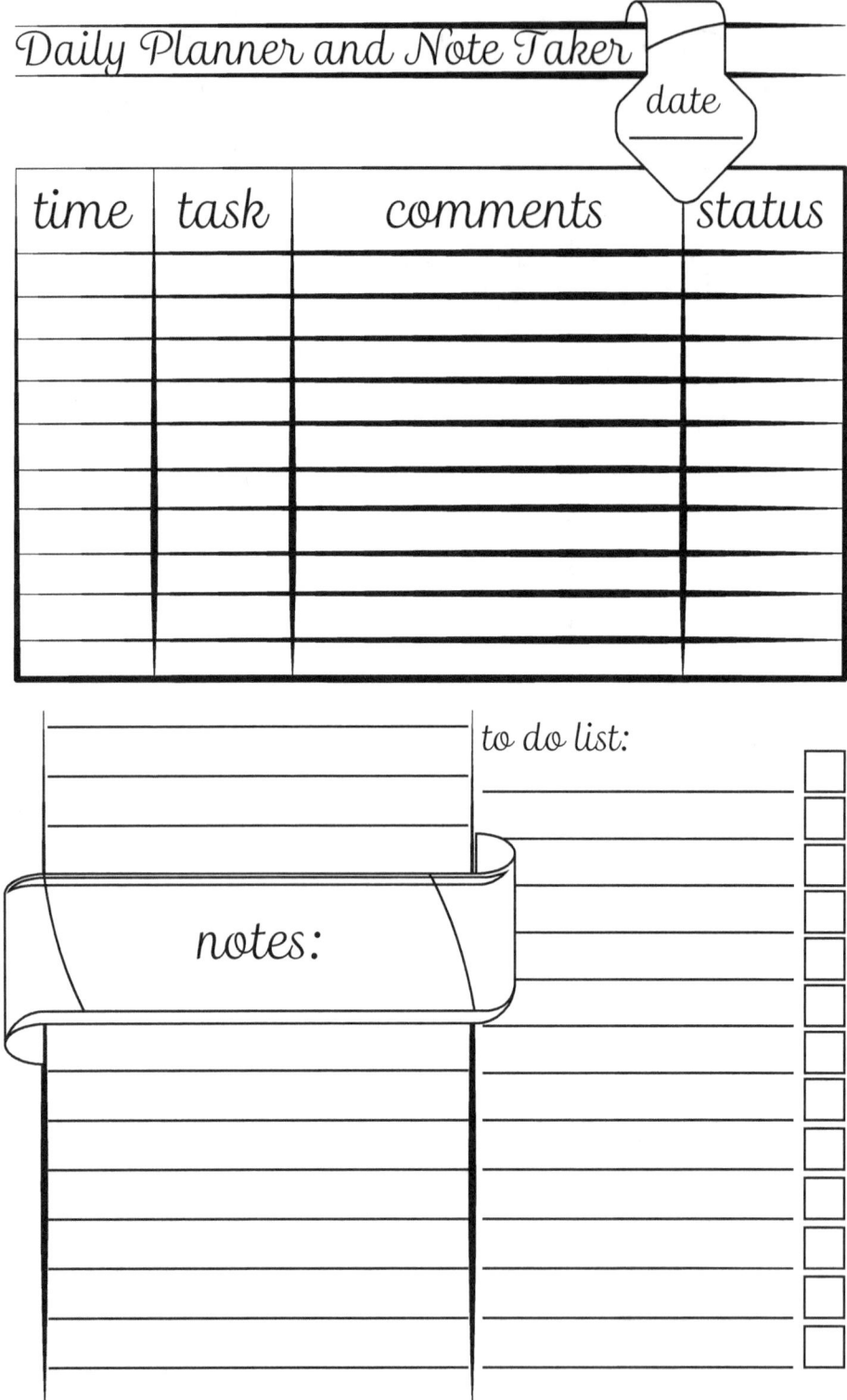

Daily Planner and Note Taker

date

time	task	comments	status

to do list:

notes:

Daily Planner and Note Taker

date
___

time	task	comments	status

to do list:

notes:

☐
☐
☐
☐
☐
☐
☐
☐
☐
☐
☐
☐
☐

Daily Planner and Note Taker

date
_____

time	task	comments	status

to do list:

notes:

- ☐
- ☐
- ☐
- ☐
- ☐
- ☐
- ☐
- ☐
- ☐
- ☐
- ☐
- ☐

Daily Planner and Note Taker

date
___

time	task	comments	status

notes:

to do list:

- ☐
- ☐
- ☐
- ☐
- ☐
- ☐
- ☐
- ☐
- ☐
- ☐
- ☐
- ☐
- ☐

Daily Planner and Note Taker

date
___

time	task	comments	status

to do list:

notes:

- ☐
- ☐
- ☐
- ☐
- ☐
- ☐
- ☐
- ☐
- ☐
- ☐
- ☐
- ☐
- ☐

Daily Planner and Note Taker

date
_____

time	task	comments	status

to do list:

notes:

Daily Planner and Note Taker

date
_____

time	task	comments	status

to do list:

notes:

☐
☐
☐
☐
☐
☐
☐
☐
☐
☐
☐
☐

Daily Planner and Note Taker

date
___

time	task	comments	status

to do list:

notes:

- ☐
- ☐
- ☐
- ☐
- ☐
- ☐
- ☐
- ☐
- ☐
- ☐
- ☐
- ☐
- ☐

Daily Planner and Note Taker

date
_____

time	task	comments	status

to do list:

notes:

Daily Planner and Note Taker

date
___

time	task	comments	status

to do list:

notes:

☐
☐
☐
☐
☐
☐
☐
☐
☐
☐
☐
☐
☐
☐

Daily Planner and Note Taker

date

time	task	comments	status

to do list:

notes:

Daily Planner and Note Taker

date
___

time	task	comments	status

to do list:

notes:

- ☐
- ☐
- ☐
- ☐
- ☐
- ☐
- ☐
- ☐
- ☐
- ☐
- ☐
- ☐
- ☐

Daily Planner and Note Taker

date
___

time	task	comments	status

to do list:

notes:

- ☐
- ☐
- ☐
- ☐
- ☐
- ☐
- ☐
- ☐
- ☐
- ☐
- ☐
- ☐
- ☐

Daily Planner and Note Taker

date
___

time	task	comments	status

to do list:

notes:

Daily Planner and Note Taker

date
___

time	task	comments	status

to do list:

notes:

Daily Planner and Note Taker

date
___

time	task	comments	status

to do list:

notes:

Daily Planner and Note Taker

date ___

time	task	comments	status

to do list:

□
□
□
□
□
□
□
□
□
□
□
□
□
□

notes:

Daily Planner and Note Taker

date
___

time	task	comments	status

to do list:

notes:

Daily Planner and Note Taker

date _____

time	task	comments	status

to do list:

notes:

- ☐
- ☐
- ☐
- ☐
- ☐
- ☐
- ☐
- ☐
- ☐
- ☐
- ☐
- ☐
- ☐
- ☐

Daily Planner and Note Taker

date
_____

time	task	comments	status

to do list:

notes:

Daily Planner and Note Taker

date
_____

time	task	comments	status

to do list:

notes:

□
□
□
□
□
□
□
□
□
□
□
□

Daily Planner and Note Taker

date _____

time	task	comments	status

to do list:

notes:

☐
☐
☐
☐
☐
☐
☐
☐
☐
☐
☐
☐
☐
☐

Daily Planner and Note Taker

date
___

time	task	comments	status

to do list:

notes:

☐
☐
☐
☐
☐
☐
☐
☐
☐
☐
☐
☐
☐
☐

Daily Planner and Note Taker

date
_____

time	task	comments	status

to do list:

notes:

Daily Planner and Note Taker

date ___

time	task	comments	status

to do list:

notes:

- ☐
- ☐
- ☐
- ☐
- ☐
- ☐
- ☐
- ☐
- ☐
- ☐
- ☐
- ☐
- ☐

Daily Planner and Note Taker

date _____

time	task	comments	status

to do list:

notes:

☐
☐
☐
☐
☐
☐
☐
☐
☐
☐
☐
☐
☐
☐

Daily Planner and Note Taker

date
_____

time	task	comments	status

to do list:

notes:

Daily Planner and Note Taker

date
_____

time	task	comments	status

to do list:

notes:

- ☐
- ☐
- ☐
- ☐
- ☐
- ☐
- ☐
- ☐
- ☐
- ☐
- ☐
- ☐
- ☐
- ☐

Daily Planner and Note Taker

date
___

time	task	comments	status

to do list:

notes:

Daily Planner and Note Taker

date
_____

time	task	comments	status

to do list:

notes:

Daily Planner and Note Taker

date
_____

time	task	comments	status

to do list:

notes:

- [ ]
- [ ]
- [ ]
- [ ]
- [ ]
- [ ]
- [ ]
- [ ]
- [ ]
- [ ]
- [ ]
- [ ]
- [ ]

Daily Planner and Note Taker

date
___

time	task	comments	status

to do list:

notes:

- ☐
- ☐
- ☐
- ☐
- ☐
- ☐
- ☐
- ☐
- ☐
- ☐
- ☐
- ☐
- ☐

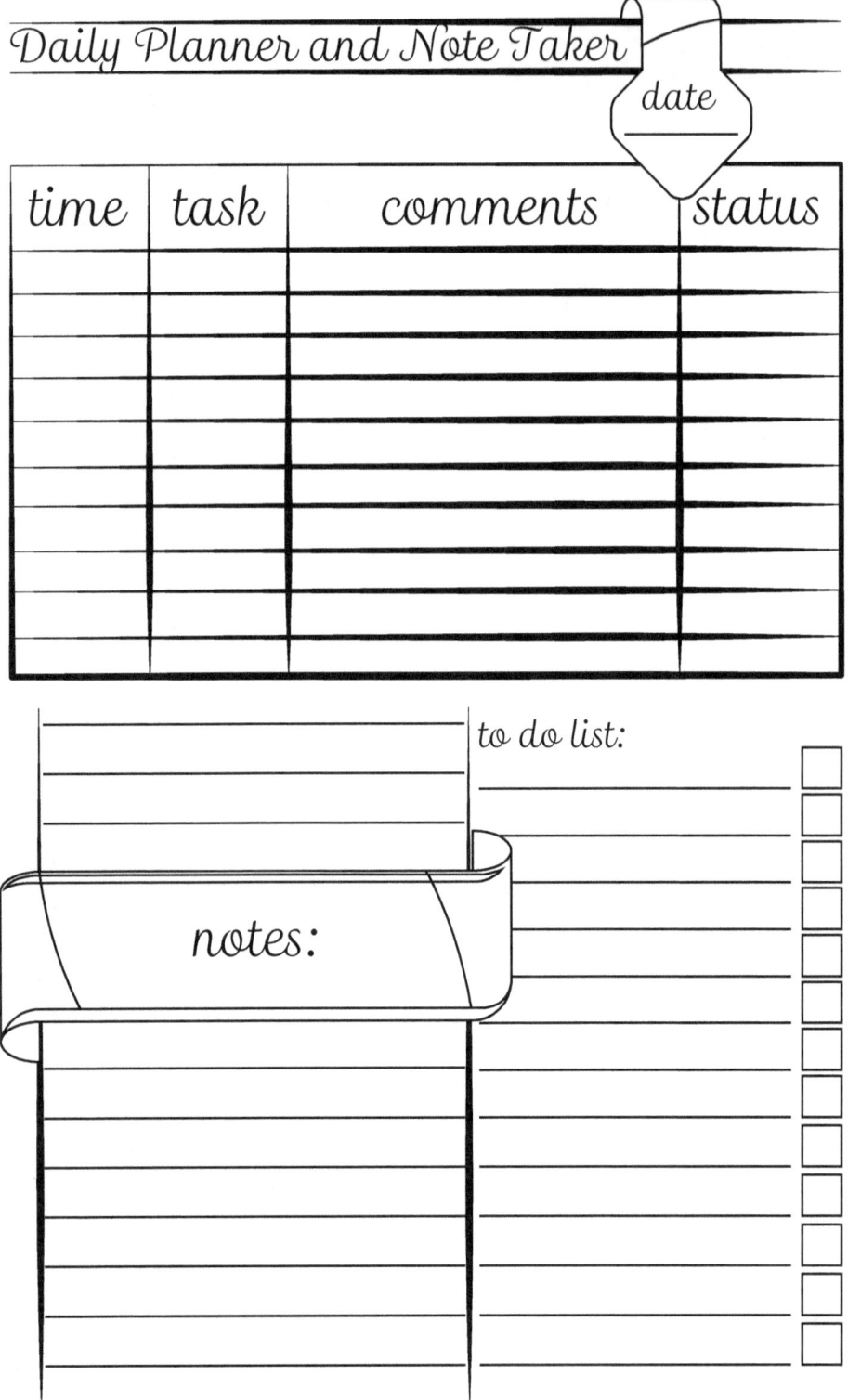

Daily Planner and Note Taker

date
___

time	task	comments	status

to do list:

notes:

Daily Planner and Note Taker

date
___

time	task	comments	status

to do list:

notes:

☐
☐
☐
☐
☐
☐
☐
☐
☐
☐
☐
☐
☐

Daily Planner and Note Taker

date
___

time	task	comments	status

to do list:

notes:

Daily Planner and Note Taker

date
___

time	task	comments	status

to do list:

notes:

Daily Planner and Note Taker

date
_____

time	task	comments	status

to do list:

notes:

- [ ]
- [ ]
- [ ]
- [ ]
- [ ]
- [ ]
- [ ]
- [ ]
- [ ]
- [ ]
- [ ]
- [ ]
- [ ]

Daily Planner and Note Taker

date
_____

time	task	comments	status

to do list:

notes:

- ☐
- ☐
- ☐
- ☐
- ☐
- ☐
- ☐
- ☐
- ☐
- ☐
- ☐
- ☐
- ☐
- ☐

Daily Planner and Note Taker

date
___

time	task	comments	status

to do list:

notes:

□
□
□
□
□
□
□
□
□
□
□
□

Daily Planner and Note Taker

date
___

time	task	comments	status

to do list:

notes:

- ☐
- ☐
- ☐
- ☐
- ☐
- ☐
- ☐
- ☐
- ☐
- ☐
- ☐
- ☐
- ☐

Daily Planner and Note Taker

date
_____

time	task	comments	status

_____

to do list:

_____ ☐

notes:

☐
☐
☐
☐
☐
☐
☐
☐
☐
☐
☐
☐

Daily Planner and Note Taker

date
___

time	task	comments	status

to do list:

notes:

☐
☐
☐
☐
☐
☐
☐
☐
☐
☐
☐
☐
☐
☐
☐

Daily Planner and Note Taker

date ___

time	task	comments	status

to do list:

notes:

Daily Planner and Note Taker

date
___

time	task	comments	status

to do list:

notes:

- [ ]
- [ ]
- [ ]
- [ ]
- [ ]
- [ ]
- [ ]
- [ ]
- [ ]
- [ ]
- [ ]
- [ ]

Daily Planner and Note Taker

date _____

time	task	comments	status

to do list:

notes:

Daily Planner and Note Taker

date
_____

time	task	comments	status

to do list:

notes:

Daily Planner and Note Taker

date
___

time	task	comments	status

to do list:

notes:

☐
☐
☐
☐
☐
☐
☐
☐
☐
☐
☐
☐

Daily Planner and Note Taker

date
_____

time	task	comments	status

to do list:

notes:

Daily Planner and Note Taker

date
___

time	task	comments	status

to do list:

notes:

- ☐
- ☐
- ☐
- ☐
- ☐
- ☐
- ☐
- ☐
- ☐
- ☐
- ☐
- ☐
- ☐

Daily Planner and Note Taker

date _____

time	task	comments	status

to do list:

notes:

- ☐
- ☐
- ☐
- ☐
- ☐
- ☐
- ☐
- ☐
- ☐
- ☐
- ☐
- ☐
- ☐
- ☐

Daily Planner and Note Taker

date _____

time	task	comments	status

to do list:

notes:

- ☐
- ☐
- ☐
- ☐
- ☐
- ☐
- ☐
- ☐
- ☐
- ☐
- ☐
- ☐

Daily Planner and Note Taker

date
_____

time	task	comments	status

to do list:

notes:

- ☐
- ☐
- ☐
- ☐
- ☐
- ☐
- ☐
- ☐
- ☐
- ☐
- ☐
- ☐
- ☐
- ☐

Daily Planner and Note Taker

date
_____

time	task	comments	status

to do list:

notes:

□
□
□
□
□
□
□
□
□
□
□
□
□
□

Daily Planner and Note Taker

date
___

time	task	comments	status

to do list:

☐
☐
☐
☐
☐
☐
☐
☐
☐
☐
☐
☐
☐
☐
☐

notes:

Daily Planner and Note Taker

date _____

time	task	comments	status

to do list:

notes:

☐
☐
☐
☐
☐
☐
☐
☐
☐
☐
☐
☐
☐

Daily Planner and Note Taker

date
___

time	task	comments	status

to do list:

notes:

☐
☐
☐
☐
☐
☐
☐
☐
☐
☐
☐
☐
☐

Daily Planner and Note Taker

date ___

time	task	comments	status

to do list:

notes:

Daily Planner and Note Taker

date
___

time	task	comments	status

to do list:

☐
☐
☐
☐
☐
☐
☐
☐
☐
☐
☐
☐
☐
☐

notes:

Daily Planner and Note Taker

date _____

time	task	comments	status

_____

to do list:

_____ ☐
_____ ☐
_____ ☐
_____ ☐
_____ ☐
_____ ☐
_____ ☐
_____ ☐
_____ ☐
_____ ☐
_____ ☐
_____ ☐
_____ ☐
_____ ☐

notes:

Daily Planner and Note Taker

date
___

time	task	comments	status

to do list:

notes:

☐
☐
☐
☐
☐
☐
☐
☐
☐
☐
☐
☐
☐

Daily Planner and Note Taker

date
_____

time	task	comments	status

to do list:

notes:

□
□
□
□
□
□
□
□
□
□
□
□
□
□

Daily Planner and Note Taker

date
___

time	task	comments	status

to do list:

notes:

☐
☐
☐
☐
☐
☐
☐
☐
☐
☐
☐
☐
☐

Daily Planner and Note Taker

date
___

time	task	comments	status

to do list:

notes:

Daily Planner and Note Taker

date
_____

time	task	comments	status

to do list:

notes:

☐
☐
☐
☐
☐
☐
☐
☐
☐
☐
☐
☐
☐

Daily Planner and Note Taker

date
_____

time	task	comments	status

to do list:

notes:

☐
☐
☐
☐
☐
☐
☐
☐
☐
☐
☐
☐
☐
☐

Daily Planner and Note Taker

date
___

time	task	comments	status

to do list:

☐
☐
☐
☐
☐
☐
☐
☐
☐
☐
☐
☐
☐

notes: